Road to Duncan

Joyce Benvenuto

Up On Big Rock Poetry Series
SHIPWRECKT BOOKS PUBLISHING COMPANY
Minnesota

IN®
DIE

Cover photo by Joyce Benvenuto
Cover & interior design by Shipwreckt Books

to Buck and Lee
　　　and all their
descendants

1. Buck and Jewel

Road to Duncan

Introduction to the Southwest

I used to pile into the breakfast nook across from my dad a long time ago. We lived in Detroit. He would have an atlas out, and it would be turned to the pages of the Southwest. I would sit and follow his words as I read upside-down the many places where he had been. He told me stories about Dallas, El Paso, the Arizona rocks, Yuma, and the California coast. He longed to be there again. He loved the heat, the dryness, the desert, the mountains—it was his endless daydream of remembered adventure.

I did not know then, that 40 years later, my daughter would be living in Arizona, my son in Texas, and I would be visiting them on a yearly basis. At first, I would only stay 10 days with my daughter; I was a teacher, and it would be my school break.

But then I retired, and my stays in Arizona grew longer until now 20 years later, I am a winter resident for more than two months at a time. I have friends there, an apartment, a library card. Likewise, Texas. I don't stay as long, but I have been traveling there too for 20 years, and I have learned the hill country from north of Austin to San Antonio.

Even more so, as I have learned the lay of the land, I have realized that these are the same Southern Pacific railroad tracks that my father traveled as a hobo. I now look at the boxcars on the sidings in Globe, Arizona, and Austin, Texas. I look for an open door. I am hoping to find a hobo inside. I never do. In the old days they were called tramps. My dad used neither of these words. He called it "going on the bum." So there you have it: my dad was a bum.

Nowadays I realize that there are really only a few ways through the mountains. So if you travel Interstate 10, you can see the train tracks running the same route as the highway. Ditto those who came before the train tracks. The historical stagecoach stop in Dragoon is not far from the present train tracks, and I-10 can be seen in the distance. So there are layers of stories to be told.

In the breakfast nook in Detroit, my father kept us fascinated on winter days. We believed him—that was it. Buck was a great storyteller. Which brings this introduction to me. I too am a storyteller. My tales entertain my children and my grandchildren. They too, now in their own time, are learning to live a life of adventure and more so, are learning to tell stories. And beyond my own family, other people of the Southwest have shared their stories about their own way through the mountains.

So I have tried to include everyone in this book: all of us on our own journeys; all of us fulfilling our own lives. I include the original people, the Apache, and the first settlers, the Mexicans. To me, they are the Southwest along with the mountains and desert. And in the midst of this spectacular scene, I have put my own family over time. We have all earned our space in the big picture.

2. San Xavier

Part One
Call of the West

3. View from Ida's pond.

Riding the Rails—The Story

It was cold. The three brothers slept in an upstairs bedroom where there was no heat. Snow could be seen through the chinks in the timber wall. Each night, the boys fought over which one would get the middle of the bed. Life was a hardship way up north. The chickens did not lay. Everyone received one egg on Christmas morning brought from afar. The nine eggs for the nine children were promptly scrambled for breakfast. That was Christmas.

So that is how Buck grew up. My dad was 16 years old in 1919. He lived in Calumet, Michigan at the tiptop of the Keweenaw Peninsula. The southern winds called. He hopped a train and headed south through Wisconsin to Chicago. To him, Chicago was warm. There he found work in the stockyards. Men were needed to ride the empty cars back to Dallas. Once in Dallas, cattle were loaded into the 20 stalls of each cattle car. Someone was paid to ride the cattle back up to the stockyards. This would be my dad. He needed to see that the cattle stayed standing for the three-day ride. He did not eat through the trip.

When he arrived in Chicago at dawn, he would be starved. He took his pay, and then ran for the all-night dinner, now serving breakfast. Flapjacks and hot coffee. More flapjacks and eggs. It was his first big, real paying job. Sausage and bacon for an extra three dimes.

He did it more than once before Dallas began to work its charm. He loved the baking heat. But he felt the call of even further west. There was work and money in the oilfields. Buck was strong. He could lay oil line. He could pick up extra money fighting in the oil camp prizefights on Friday nights. No boxing gloves. With no neck and long arms, he could fight and win. But the call of further west was strong. So he moved on. Out there was San Antonio, El Paso, the California coast.

In El Paso, he was caught in the railroad yards and put in jail for vagrancy. By then he had a partner to ride the rails. His name was Lee. Lee carved monkeys and baskets out of the peach and plum pits left over from their jail cell meal. Nowadays they call this hobo art. But the railroad needed hands to lay down railroad line. So Lee and my dad were put on the chain gang to hammer down spikes into the railroad ties. The gang boss would call the step. Altogether now—the hammer down, step to the next, and the chains kept tune.

4. Lizard.

Once free, he looked further west. Arizona framed his two favorite words: hot and dry. He was good now at riding trains. He could ride on top a boxcar. He could hop from car to car. He could jump from one boxcar top to another passing train.

After Yuma, in the Imperial Valley, they needed money once more. They joined the pickers of the lettuce crop. It was hot. The unwashed lettuce that he ate made his stomach-ache, so once more he moved on.

Ahh California, the coast at last, and the trains went north. He followed the coast. In Washington, he worked in the lumber camps. He mastered the axe and bucksaw with easy strength.

Then, on to Montana and the wheat fields. He could work into the fall. And when the crops were in, he hopped another train going east and home. This time it was now Detroit where the family had moved south to work in the auto industry. He was happy to see his younger brothers and sister until the chill of Michigan brought in snow. It was the remembered cold. Then Buck could be seen down near the rail yard roundhouse looking for an open boxcar door. And without a word of goodbye, he would be gone for another time. His dad would shake his head. He couldn't tie his son to the porch pillars. He had to let him go.

Between the ages of 16 and 26, Buck rode the rails out west three times. One trip would take three years. He knew the way. He knew the stops. He knew the heat.

It was enough adventure for a lifetime.

5. Buck.

Spokane!

Southern Pa...

R.R.————

Cal

Az

New Mexic

Divide

Yuma

Tucson

Safford

Duncan

Willcox

El Paso

6. Map A: Southern Pacific Railroad - Detroit to Spokane

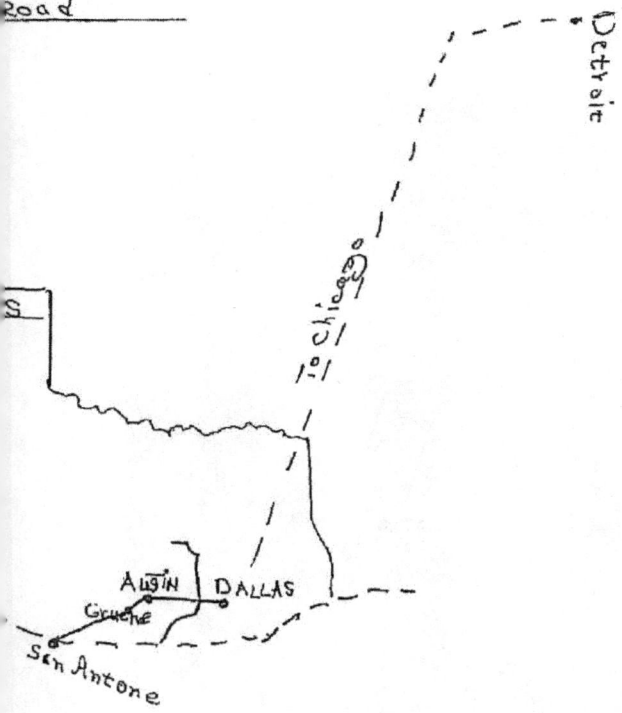

Road

S

To Chicago

Detroit

Augin   Dallas
Gruene
San Antone

7. Boxcar.

Hot and Dry

Rolling wheels, hitch of wheels
hitting coupled track, leaving Dallas,
heading for Fort Worth, 50 cars long
and then Chicago bound.
Inside each car, 40 steers
with a center row to feed and tend
and each end held a place for a man
to mind the steers.
(this was his job for three days each run).
      Rolling wheels.

They hit Chicago before dawn
where Buck ate his fill to forget three days
of sucking air, the smell of longhorns,
straw picking at his legs. Water from a pail.

Gut full, he walked the streets, saw dawn
rise up over steel girders, walked a pier.
Gulls overhead, the North wind blew
at the back of his neck. Buck shivered.
Then memory brought him Texas heat, sun
on his eyelids, his hat brim low.

Maybe three, four hours in the North
by the emerald lake, its wind, its waves
before he was back at the train yard
looking 'round for a slow-moving freight,
looking for the roll of wheels heading south,
an open box car door, some straw for long sleep.

His steps matched the accelerating, creeping pace.
Last seen, the blank open square of a box car door
at a crossing gate, rolling toward Dallas, Texas heat.

The Gandy Dancer

Vagrants, a missed move in the railroad yard.
The detective nailed them, Buck and Lee,
their wandering on pause this one more time.

—Yes, locked in the El Paso jail
saving their apricot stones
for carving later when they were free.
And for now—the chain gang.
Step fast and move on as one, altogether men,
so the locked steel did not make their ankles bleed.
The chains were their song in rhyme
dancing from railroad tie to railroad tie
       repairing line.

—To be a gandy dancer ... Buck laughed,
said it improved his dancing moves,
because later on, in future years,
cleaned up, he hit the dance halls.
       Hello, to Gruene, that's north of San Antone.
       Women loved him, his two-step smooth.
       His hand on slim waists, a guiding smile
       rounding the dance floor. Fiddle bows moved.

But for now, thirty days served, and they were free.
Lee's back to the yammering wall of the railroad car,
his deft hand carved eyes, a mouth, a small monkey.
My dad pulled his denim cap down and dreamed,
listening to the rhythm of the clacking wheels...
through Lordsburg, through Benson, through Yuma, yes,
and then—straight up the California shore, free
boxcar bums, 1924. A road more open
than Whitman dreamed, and in between,
       they walked.

Jail Time in Texas

Locked in the El Paso jail,
steel bar doors shut fast
behind his back: Vagrancy, 1924
...a pillow of chain link springs,
a convict jacket, a stamped number back,

confined in steel,
                    reinforced.
Night cooled, then sweat damp, three times a day.

...Dreams of pissing on running roaches,
rows of bars to count each day,
green peas to count and roll on a plate
...or counting silver centipede legs divine...

My father was released in time.
But a Texas jail

                    locks forever

                           inside a man.

Hop a Train—1924

Wheels in their eyes set them a go.
Run along the accelerating train,
boxcar ladder near at hand. One arm reached while still running;
one hand on the ladder rung; one swing pulled Buck up and away;
head high and feet from solid ground. Lee did the same.

Glorious ride atop boxcar roof. Arizona mountains
after the Continental Divide. Sun-squint to the distance.
Lost hat. Willcox in 400 miles—a siding where they might slip in
an open boxcar door to sleep like children on cattle straw.

Wake up. Where are they? Why it's rattlesnake crafts for sale,
a square store on the desert floor behind a yard of strung poles
         holding a tale of found junk—strung
across wire lines where the wind rules, blows a symphony
through and about hanging pots and pans of miners,
colanders, spatulas, imagined tales of mistakes made,
         a slip of the foot...diamondback surprise.
It is all moving metal motion, clanging, clanging time.
And swaying skulls,
         pelvic bones blown smooth.
                  They are now wind toys.

Here rules the rattlesnake. His skin has become craft
in the gift shop, an emporium of eyeglass cases, headbands,
the wallet Lee always wished he had.
The two touch wind, touch rust, touch the rattlesnake...

         But they are railroad bums...hungry for days
         ...so hop back on the outgoing train,
traveling westward, dreaming of jam on toast, jumping
from boxcar roof to moving boxcar roof, their eyes
on the mountains, sharp, stark horizon, looking
for that break in the ridge line, familiar rocks.

Lee touched his wallet. Buck took his glasses from their case.

And Many Have Entertained Angels, Unaware

When you are hungry and homeless, you take chances.
You arrive at back doors of houses. You knock at doors
near trash bins of restaurants. But folks hate the hobo,
my father. They sic dogs on him. They shoot guns.
       They treat him like rodent.

Like a desert rat, the hobo combs the horizon.
It is 1929. The parasites from field lettuce
gnaw at his gut. There, on the horizon, this hobo,
my father sees the Okie fires. He rejoices. Oh,
to have the religion of Okies. He makes his way
on bone dead knees to the ring of family voices.
The women and children have begged today
       at the bakeries, at the houses.
And they have been given bread—it is
       the glory chain of the Okie trail—
for people feed the Okies, gentleness of women
and children, sober eyes, whispered thanks.

Now, like a magnet, my father finds them.
       And they welcome him to the fire,
because everyone who sits at the Okie fire
       is fed. It is their religion.

It is a desert night. More stars are in the sky
than can be imagined. There is fire light on the faces.
Someone is telling a story about angels and exodus,
       about chariots.

          ❧

Which brings me to the following day and my father.
It's eastern California…
Tomorrow's train on the horizon is coming up behind him
       as he walks the rails.

A Crack of Light—1929

In a California train yard, asleep
in a boxcar, they were careless.
The railroad detective heard their noise,
said, *You sons-of-bitches, I'll fix you good,*
and rolled shut the steel box door.
Whistling, he slid the outside bolt in place.

They yelled; they pounded
the walls, but the footsteps moved away,
and they were left
until they heard, the boxcar coupled and moved,
coupled again, and moved again…
Then faster and faster the rock 'n' roll…

on their way somewhere; they lived in the bar of light
at the crack of the door, mile after mile.
The crack grew dark; grew light; grew dark three times
to the rock 'n' roll of hunger, of thirst
as they went ahead and peed. As they curled listless
at watching the miles at the crack of the door
of this day and the next day and the next of their lives.

They stopped somewhere cold. They were rolled backward,
uncoupled. They heard silence. A bird.
They guessed another railroad yard. They hit the doors.
Lee had a blade of a saw. They tried to cut a hole.
No good. Not this time Lee. Time to pray.

Then a small boy going to school
heard and yelled, *Ma, Ma, there's people in that car.*
Help!
She heard too. A mom in overalls. She grabbed
a steel ruler from her bib-pocket just in case
she had to whack some heads.
She released the bolt and slid the door
where the small boy stared at the bums, their straw hair,

their pale breath, their watering eyes.
Kid, what town, we in? and *California's where we been.*

This here's Spokane. You're up in Washington.

Well, blow me down. Their heads bowed low.
Thank you, mam.

That wasn't the first my dad nearly died.
That wasn't even the last.
But somehow there's always been a crack of light
at the edge of a door
a small child's bright eyes full of wonder...

a bum still quick inside.

8. Cowboys at the Triangle-T

Blue Denim

Long after my dad was a bum,
and I was born and almost raised,
sitting beside him watching
The Lone Ranger on our black and white
16 inch screen, he would give a start,
point and yell at the old T.V.
There's my rocks! There they are!
It was an oft-used movie set we would see,
large boulders for a backdrop—for a gunfight,
or a meeting of railroad thieves.
Sublime Arizona scene—those house size rocks,
and then close-up—Tonto pivots,
a slow rattler rising, coiled to strike.

Years later, I'm here, just off Interstate 10.
I think my dad might know this place.
boulders left for eons, dusty suns, white crane moons.
And I stand and listen. The bartender at the Triangle-T
tells customers—this place was used for movie sets,
so I go out and walk about the Arizona blue
looking for a Hollywood movie scene,
squinting memory into present.
Did one stand there or there to get that pose?
I listen for the rattlesnake, but feel
only bee hum heat and thirsty sun.

Searching...I look for a tramp shaking sleep from his hair,
denim jacket, hunkering down in busted boots,
his arm reaching out with pliers
for a pan in the fire.

I still have his pocket watch.
I turn a full 360 degrees,

                    winding my time.

Third Grade

The first time I was in trouble
was in the Third Grade, and we were told
we were going to learn to write an essay.
The topic was to be *My Father.* I burned.
My left-hand pencil flew across the page.
My father was a chain gang bum in Texas
were my starting words.
That would get interest; I was sure.
I told of his adventures—how
once locked in a refrigerator car,
he ate oranges for a day. He was so cold
when finally they opened the door,
he gulped the golden heat into his bones.

My essay was red flagged (though I did not know
what that could mean). My teacher shared my words
with the principal who was concerned...
and called my mom
            to come and have a conversation
            about imagination in a growing child.
            Mom was floored when she read the words,
            her face flushed, her hands fluttered as she turned
            the page.
This is her father, she apologized.
He tells her stories, and she believes they are true.
Then I tried to say that they were true, but to no avail.
My mom, my teacher, and the principal decreed
there and then I was a highly excitable child
so should be entertained with mellow tales
of—going to the beach and such.

That night, after I was in bed,
I could hear them in the kitchen...
You have to cut that out, she cried. *She goes to school.*
She tells these things.
So my dad was quiet after that on days when my mom

was at home. But there were other days,
long rides in the car and back...when I would ask
for more...and he would tell me true.

9. Longhorn bronze, Dallas, TX.

Detroit—1952
(Oakman and Grand River)

It was Buck's version of watching
the kids. We played in boxcars
left on the siding.
Doors open, we climbed in,
hoisting each other,
foot in hand
our bellies splayed on the boxcar floor,
legs whirligig,
until we pulled ourselves all the way up.
Whoop and holler.

Buck was lookout
for the railroad detective.
He'd know when to run.
In the distance, a circle of hobos.
Coffee smell came downwind.
Another waft too.
Buck squinted to see—and called it dope.
Those boys won't be trouble.
Not today.

Buck knew Detroit
                    and playgrounds.

The Last Great Prizefight

When he was done at 90,
Buck rested in a nursing home,
ate yogurt, still combed his white hair
into a part.

But at night, his roommate
knew demented rage, hovered
above Buck's bed, delivered blows.

Two a.m. bed-check heard the shouts,
rushed in, dragged the roommate off,
called in help to end it all.

In the morning I received the call,
apologies for the incident, attempts to explain
the unexpected scene.

Enraged, we rushed the hall,
my father bruised at forearm, forehead, hands.
This cannot be true, we meant to scream,
a madman roommate left with dad.

But last, we heard my father's view.
His blue eyes—lit with excitement,
his telling rapid, his voice tripped…
I got to fend his blows. My arm blocked his right.
I swung and landed … one or two.

The nursing home moved my dad that day
to a far wing room with a gentle man
and a kinder voice.

So you see, this is how
my dad died: hematoma still
raised on his forehead, his hand, a web
of busted veins.

I grieved, but in some way I knew
my dad went out with knuckles raised,
his head down to protect his chin,
crafting one more blow.

10. Peach pit monkey.

11. Rail crossing.

Part Two
Time backward and time forward

12. Pillar Rock.

The Apache Story

The Apache lands are roughly 1/6 of the state of Arizona. Most of it is pristine wilderness. By being uncompromising, the Apache have saved for the American people a unique look into the past— what it was like before the conquest of White men began.

It is true that the Apache were brutal, unkind to both Spanish and Anglos. This is why there are few architectural sites to visit in southeast Arizona, no pueblos, no missions, no quaint Spanish or cowboy towns. The Apache burned it all. True, there is the magnificent St. Xavier Mission below Tucson, but that is another tribe of Native Americans who own a good piece of the Arizona border.

White history begins with the trail to California which began somewhere before Texas, across New Mexico, along the Chiricahua Mountains of Arizona, and across the desert to the pass on the California coast and San Diego. In Arizona, a wagon train, a Butterfield stagecoach or pony express had to stop at prescribed water holes—springs—and get all the water they could if they expected to make it across the parched expanse. The rivers and washes could dry up in drought times, but never the springs.

Enter Cochise, the great Apache chief in the mid-1800s. He knew keenly that he controlled the prized water. So he bartered with each traveler. His preference was rifles. He would trade other things as well, but what he wanted most were bullets and guns. Nobody died. The trade would happen. Apache Spring gave endless water, enough to get everyone over the flats to the next spring in the Dragoon Mountains where perhaps more Apache might be waiting. Cochise did this for more than 20 years.

Then the United States Government decided that none of this was allowed. Cochise could not control the desert; nobody told the government what to do. Thus, the war began.

Cochise outwitted soldiers to the end. His chiefdom was then passed on to Geronimo, an equally cagey warrior who in turn held off the government troops for another 20 years. At the end, he did surrender because of the suffering of Apache women and children. He and his men would have fought it out to the death.

The U. S. Government then forced the tribe from their Chiricahua homeland to a reservation, up to the north, a remote spot in the mountains on the Gila River. On the San Carlos Rez, there are still those who claim to be relatives of Geronimo. Apache is still spoken by the tribe.

Like any culture that is uprooted from its homeland, the Apache floundered in their new surroundings. For instance, the Apache attached the stories of their culture to various rock formations in the Chiricahua Mountains. An Apache could point to a rock and tell a story important to the moral teachings of the tribe. The young ones

learned the stories and retold them to their own children. When the Apache were torn from their homeland, they were torn from their stories, the spiritual connections that gave the tribe sustaining values.

Having said all this, I offer you these following poems. They have been written over the 20 years that I have visited San Carlos, and reflect, I hope, my understanding of Apache culture. At some point a young Apache will start to fill notebooks full of writing and emerge as the great storyteller of the tribe.

And as the reader may have started to guess, it was the Apache who knew the trail across the desert, followed by the settlers; followed by the Southern Pacific Railroad which carried my dad on his railroad journeys; followed by Interstate 10 which I now take on a regular basis to get to Tucson or east to Silver City, New Mexico. It's the same way through the mountain passes and across the desert for all of us—time backward and time forward.

13. Saguaro cacti.

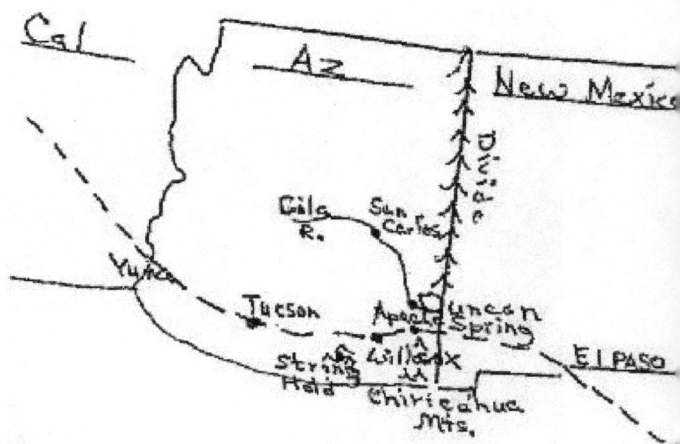

Southern Pac
Butterfield St
R.R. — — — —

Cal
Az
New Mexico
Divide
Gila R.
San Carlos
Yuma
Tucson
Apache
Duncan Spring
String Hold
Willcox
Chiricahua Mts.
El Paso

14. Map B: The Apache Lands.

Road - 1865
Mail - 1857.

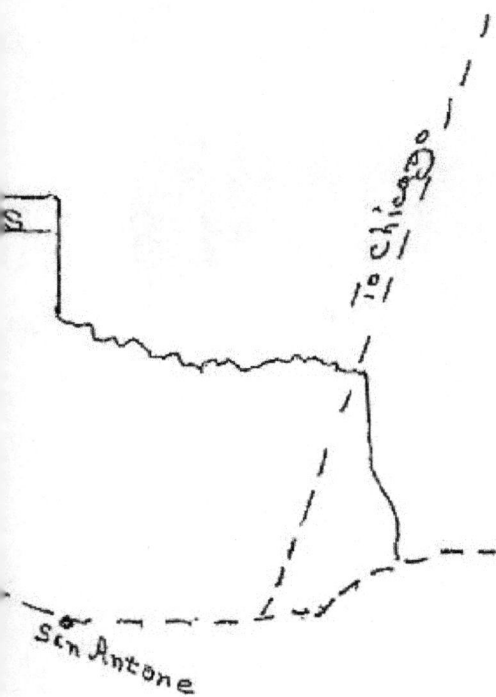

To Chicago

S.

San Antone

15. Apache lands in the distance, source of Gila River.

Acorn Soup

The Apache women gather near
as I lift my spoon,
their jet eyes bright
as my own expectation.
The soup smells sharp of desert oak,
and the taste has the tang of acorns.
The color is of yellow squash
and high-desert sunset.
I dip my warm fry bread.

They talk of the acorn gathering ...
along the Gila on a Saturday morning
before the mountain snows.
Five sisters in jeans and camp dresses
bending low from the waist,
their brown hands
in motion from earth to reed baskets.

1,000 acorns, at least, to satisfy.

Now they bring out the jars
of soft acorn flour, golden-hued,
and I listen to transformations
from hard nut to season's food,
and now we are chattering and interrupting
about pork-back at Safeway.

It is a Rez twilight with no agenda
other than scratch cooking ...
and smiles when secrets are revealed.

Others drop in.
The breath of soup is greeting,
knowing a bowl will be offered ...
            with rising moon fry bread.

Apache in Camp Dresses

(going to a luncheon conference)

❧

Flowers of the high desert
in colors of green, blooming vine,
first rose dawn, low melon sunset.

Loose at the waist and bust,
long cotton skirts, ankles
glimpsed in light wind,
striding motion
brushing white dust.
Perhaps—a long necklace,
color of turquoise tweaking
black hair.

Like nuns in a row toward chapel
like Mennonites wearing bonnets in a field
like Muslims in gold-thread scarves
                              shopping at market.

❧

Power of cloth.

The Gaan Dancers

They are dancing tonight in the rim-rock canyon
     called *The Stronghold*; men dressed
as mountain spirits, male ghost bodies painted white;
     their headdress, bonnets of woven rainbow
     on braided heads.

They jump through the popping fire.
     Sparks hit their naked chests.
To flinch would not be a man.
     To feint a jump would not be a man.
The forty drummers are ceaseless,
     rattles sound of rattlesnake,
     whips like pistol fire.
The Gaan weave above the fire lit ground,
     momentary spirits.

 The outer ring of women—
     one-step a circle around the men
        —keep the magic moving.
The beat flows through the arc of their shoulders.
     The trance completes the circle of earth.
        Night nods.
        I am there.
Behind us, children dance or sleep,
point to their own dancing fathers.
        Chalk men hold no fear.

We are all held by stars and mountain, a sky offering,
five thousand feet above the desert floor
and the miles-away light
        of store and gas pump.

Down below—at the edge of blacktop,
a hand painted sign of cardboard
        points one arrow our way.
        —*Mountain Dance*—the letters say.

You miss the sign if you drive too fast.

16. Gaan dancer.

Apache Spring

Not a dream…Apache Spring slides down the wall
of brown stone, perpetually
in the high desert. The spring holds true
when all waterholes go dry.

Water—more valuable than corn, or guns, or gold.
Held once by Cochise, leader, chief.
He set the rules for Apache Pass—wagon,
stage, the way across sand and through
mesquite to California shores.

White men needed water;
Cochise sought guns (bullets too),
so the trade went on in the narrow pass
of cottonwood, mountain lion,
singing birds, tarantula
until the government plotted: catch
the chief…lured with coffee, talk of peace.

Cochise, smarter than they, slashed his way
from the baited tent and ran
        across the sun horizon mesa
        into the rocks, pillars of stone.

Cochise held this pass twenty years.
Geronimo held it even more—
springs of manhood,
        diligence, guts, and will,
a simple spring that never stops,
sprung from a cave wall to bring desert bloom.
        ✑
It's a three-mile hike from trailhead start.
Once there, we know it is no dream…water flows.
Our outstretched fingers reach along the wall;
water flow across our hands. It is cool and fresh,
                        free.

Casino Jacket

When I wear the black jacket in Tuscon or Phoenix
an Apache will talk to me—

Hey there, you been on the Rez?
Howz it going—San Carlos? And we talk for a moment.
I tell news of the old block Bureau buildings,
the upgrade on the breakfast café,
new plastic tables outside. We chat like friends.

And I say—You need to go back up soon—but they always say—
Wish I could. Too busy—making money, the American Dream.

I wear the wrinkled jacket, though my kids say—God, No.
The gold embroidered letters have hanging threads. I wear it
shopping at Cheap Stores. Management murmurs, thinking—

This one's homeless—watch her pockets, there.

For me, it's a good fit. And the Apache approach me. It's like
I'm a touch of home. For them, the magical light from the peaks
called Three Sisters shines in the polyester cloth.
And it's ink black with gold letters like Rez night—no electric sky,
only brilliant wash of comfort stars.

Woman of Eleven Horses

Apache woman rides her horses on weekends
out to the foot of mountains or along
the spring roadsides lined with yellow blowing poppies.

Apache woman, with her wealth of girlishness still strong;
she does not bend to opinion or wishes,
no interest
       in household chores or mending clothes.

Apache woman still keeps in her heart, her girlhood
when she rode her horse to the river and standing
on its back, jumped into brown sand Gila waters,

       and with her brothers, rode out across the high desert,
       their only complaint—that she "peed" that girl way.

Apache woman, with her smile hidden on workdays
in her office, but visible should you ask

       about horses.

17. Woman of eleven horses.

Chiricahua Dawn

In the faint light
you can see the shadowed slopes exactly
from the desert floor,
knife sharp against winter.
Behind me the rock cliffs of Cochise
and I imagine he camped in my spot too.
His memories in the waking dawn
      wake here still,
        in stone rows, in stone piles,
        in shards and bones.
And I bring my memories to add…
some like desert rain,
gone as fast as they fall,
but others like rock rows along the drive
make memory book lanes too
      for me to walk again…

recollections that hold,
in the first margin of morn.

Cochise

I went to the mountain of Cochise today.
They say he is buried there, deep in a chasm.
Even today, I saw three eagles fly overhead
      circling the sky like sentinels.

I took advantage.

The three eagles meant I might have three prayers!
I was excited.
The first—I asked for rain on behalf
of every plant, the cottonwood to the thirsty rose.
My tongue pleaded—no year of parched leaves.

The second was thanksgiving—
      for birth,
my grandson of seven days—naked, soft,
his smile from the other side
      of miracle.

As for the third, I hesitated.
The asking and the thanksgiving were quite enough
      for me, now.
One doesn't want to use up all one's prayers in one day.

To be out of eagles would be terrifying.

I Found a Woman

I climbed the high mesa
where the Salado had been before, ancient people.
Once on top, I found shards inside the earthworks
and a hand-stone used for grinding,
heft tool brought by a strong arm—
some grandma, 700 years long past.

(I could sense her smell, her hide dress,
        the thin smile of her silence)

I held the stone for a long time
motioning the grinding action.
Its warmth weighed my palm and spoke to my heart.
I answered—Hello, Dearie,
        you, who held this last,
        crushing the morning corn for the pot.
        I am holding this now.

I cook too, and like you, I have no lines in my fingertips
from working flour into bread. I know
the preparation, the anticipation of feeding people,
my granddaughter's face, looking up,
secure there will be food—while she plays at my feet.

You are not erased by these past 700 years, or by the wind
blowing across this high place
or the sun endlessly drying time to dust.

Our hands embrace
        through this root stone
                and the work we do.

Sustenance

I

The minute I married an Italian, I realized
it was food that fetched him.
So not knowing a fry from a stir, I followed
my mother-in-law into her basement
near the furnace, next to the cardboard boxes
labeled wedding dress, dishes etc.,
next to the original steamer trunk—
There was the scrubbed wooden table
and scrubbed window-shade roller
that was her rolling pin. It was a sacred place,
no mice squeaking in her corners,
only Perry Como on a dial radio.

> She thought I was definitely
> not up to grade.
> My Irish fisher-woman stub of hands
> a birth defect.

But I, the famine Irish, had staying power
could last in the ring to the 9th bell,
and I worked 'til I made dough into a blister.
My wrists became fine tools,
my thumbs indenters, my forearms
engines of motion—whacking yeast,
adding olive oil,
and I became—queen of pizza.

Everyone sat at my table.
My father-in-law ate thirds.
And the aged auntie offered secrets
of subtle spice.

11.

Thirty years later, I found myself
on a high mesa of ethereal beauty
where Eva stood in her prefab house kitchen,
a braid of jet and silver down her back,
her long hands in flour (before the day's sun began).
She lifted the iron pan with ease—
The scrubbed home sat near the bend of the Gila
lined with cottonwoods and desert oak.
Robby Bee, Red Nativity, played on her Panasonic—

Here I was with the Apache at Eva's table,
those who had not spoken English for 100 years
by choice.
And they whispered jokes as they stole sly looks—
Her gap tooth may be a curse or magic.

> Like my mother-in-law,
> they thought
> I was not—much for sure.

But I was in their midst sampling fry bread.
I held up the gold texture to the hanging light.
I saw the smooth blister—
> *Ahhh, baking powder is how you get this.*
Their mouths slowed as they saw and heard
I understood the recipe.
> I smiled, taking a satisfied bite—

> *And wait, I smell lard.*
Their voices changed to English,
> *We get it from the butcher at Willcox.*
> *He holds it for us—*
> *When we travel 10, the McDonald's exit.*
I ate more than one. Fry bread for courage.
> Fry bread for strength.
> > Sustenance.

lll.

And now you see it too.

We are legion—Italian, Apache, Irish
                to whom the world has held out
                        a black potato.

We are legion
                who have figured out the end run.
We have found a cup of flour, water,
                leavening…

With our aprons tied to save our dresses,
with our soda bread recipe smudged on the counter,
with flour on our noses from shooing a fly…

                Sustenance.

18. Pow wow dancers.

19. Road to the Rez.

Medicine Purse—Four Totems

White doeskin, black Apache beads,
I wear it around my neck—for poetry.
Inside a folded note from my daughter,
(now she's middle aged)
promising a lunch—she pays—though
by now, we have had many.

Inside too, a bit of ancient sea fossil pulled
from a riverbank, a cut in the earth
near Blanco, Texas. I was there
with my sons. There, giant cephalopod tracks
still mark the river bottom, footprints in stone,
big as bathtubs going forward, telling a story
of browsing (like me through this lifetime),
huge bodies still sensed in the air.

And third, a plum pit monkey
(tramp art—see no evil, code of a hobo)
carved by the half-Indian partner of my dad,
both on a road gang to lay train track.
 Run, said the guard, *and I'll shoot you
 in the back. Go ahead, try.*
(He didn't run, so now I am here).

Ahhh, the fourth—Apache magic
is all about fours and balance.
But I say—no, not yet.
The fourth is still empty space, the vacant spot,
still waiting, still looking

 for one last totem.

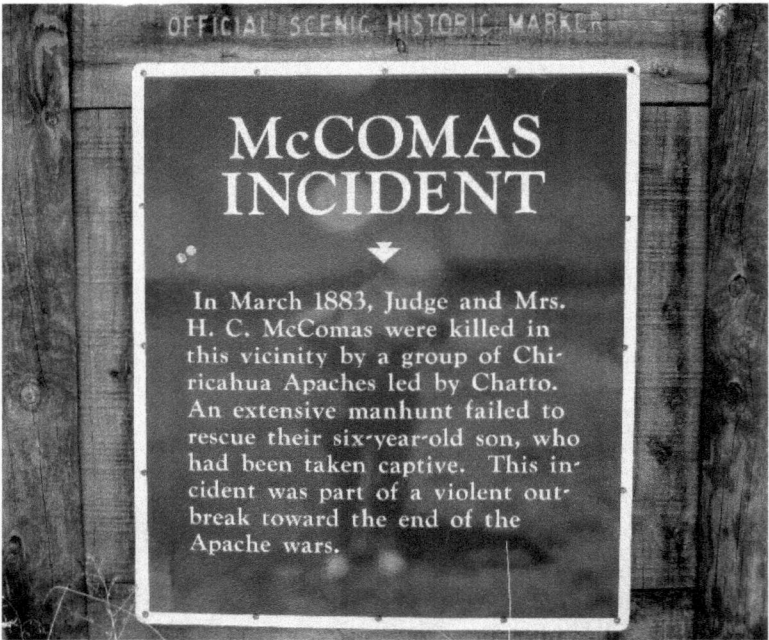

McCOMAS
INCIDENT

In March 1883, Judge and Mrs. H. C. McComas were killed in this vicinity by a group of Chiricahua Apaches led by Chatto. An extensive manhunt failed to rescue their six-year-old son, who had been taken captive. This incident was part of a violent outbreak toward the end of the Apache wars.

20. Historical marker.

Part Three
I wish all travelers well

21. Inn at Castle Rock.

Travelers—The Border Story

Bisbee Arizona is one place along the border that is sure to entertain. Take money. Not only is it a tourist spot because of its history, but it is also an art colony. This means every small shop along the street tempts the traveler with things not found in box stores, things you didn't know you wanted until you see them.

But you don't have to enter the art shops. You can simply walk along the streets and enjoy the sights of clever houses set into the cliffs or climb the many steps that take you to the top of the stone outcroppings. If you love exercise, this is the place.

But let's dig a little deeper. Let's take you to the door of the Inn at Castle Rock where immediately you see you have entered some sort of rare artful world of rooms in layers that ascend the cliff landscape. Which room is yours, you ask? Then you are led through hallways of history, each turn revealing a new setting of some genius decorator never seen on those "let's make your room pop" shows.

∽

The first time we went to Castle Rock, we knew there were ghosts, but we took a wait-and-see attitude. We were put into some sort of Egyptian Room that was set into the back-garden wall of the wooden building. The room had the least ghosts, said the young woman who showed us up. We unpacked; we went out to eat; we were tired; we crashed into bed.

Except it was hard for me to sleep. I kept having dreams of a Spanish woman with long flowing black hair, dressed in a long white dress, and bare feet standing near my bedside. The curious thing was that she had red roses falling from her shoulder to her waist in a kind of a swirl. I woke up. I used the toilet. I went back to sleep, and she returned again in my dream. That was odd—to keep dreaming of the same thing. I woke up and turned on the lamp for the rest of the night. The room was calm. Nothing to alarm, except for my daughter who wondered why I was sleeping with the lamp full on.

The next morning, we drank our dark coffee sitting on an upstairs porch at the front of the inn overlooking the street. My daughter wondered what was up with me during the night? So I told her my repeated dream. Her face changed. She said, *Oh my gosh, you saw her...,* and I said, *Who?* And then my daughter said she didn't want to tell me this because she was afraid I would freak and refuse to stay at the Rock. *What, what?,* was my reply. Well, it seems that long ago (the place is over 100 years old) a young woman was shot in the street below, and that sometimes at night she is still seen. She will stop a car, or walk in front of a car, or plead for help. The driver usually jumps from the car thinking she is real...but then she disappears.

So I asked, *Ha, what is she wearing? I bet...,* And, of course, she is wearing a long white dress and blood is covering her bosom. She has bare feet.

Now those of you who believe in overactive imaginations are pausing at this moment, but I have more to add. This time when we went to Castle Rock, we stayed in the active ghost room. By now we are seasoned warriors and totally comfortable in the place. The other two went down to breakfast, and I was left in the room.

I went out on the small, second floor porch and enjoyed the morning sun for a while. But then I decided to join them, so I went back to the screen door. The door was locked. The hook was now down and fastened. I was locked out on the porch. Fortunately the porch I was on is part of a series of connecting porches, so I was able to walk from one to another and get back around to my room. The hook was still down. I lifted it and then tried several times to jar the door so it would naturally fall into the eye. It never did.

There you have it—a second ghostly encounter. Check it out, if you dare.

22. Candles.

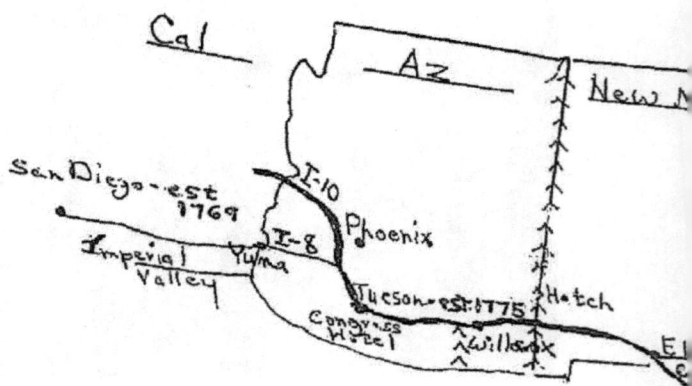

I- 10

Cal

Az

New M

San Diego--est 1769

I-10

Phoenix

I-8

Yuma

Imperial Valley

Tucson--est 1775

Hatch

Conoys.es Hotel

Willcox

E

23. Map C: I-10, the Interstate.

erstate _____

Texas

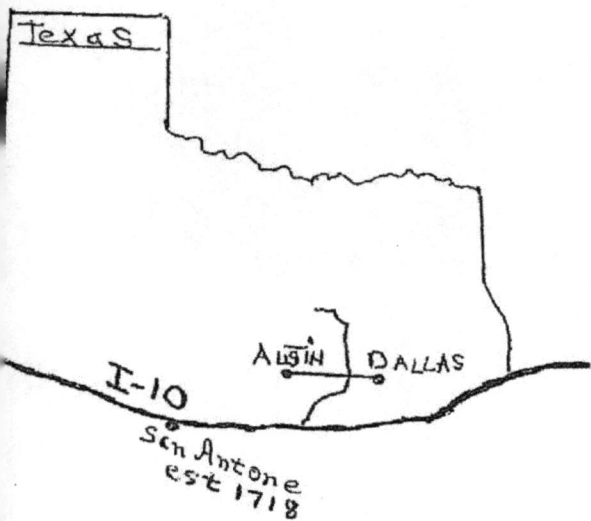

I-10

Austin   DALLAS

San Antone
est 1718

24. Red truck crossing the desert.

I-10—The Interstate (Look at the Map)

Chili peppers and tumbleweed,
      hang from road-signs,
Hatch, New Mexico, red roast of high desert.
Lordsburg next, best Mexican food ever—
      Eva, old cook, rises from her bench,
        starts her grille, her hands on tortillas.
Distant mountains stay distant in the windshield
even as we cross this mountain range.

(don't exit here, drug deal going down)

The Apache Tribe gives thanks on Thanksgiving.
On the Rez, Nina prepares beans.
Next exit, Mormon underwear—not made in China.
Down the highway, Meth-head silver trailers
      hang Christmas lights,
      look normal, get skipped by the law.
The rattlesnake hibernates; we snowbirds migrate.
Distant mountains stay distant.
      The Continental Divide behind us,
        no gas needed, all downhill.

(don't exit here: gun deal. Don't slow down—
      look straight ahead)

Our exit, Hotel Congress, Tucson.
      Water hole,
      John Dillinger died here.
Illegals, wary, eat carefully at the next table,
      other Mexicans here to help them.
Tourists with maps, talk to Carl at the front desk.
On the street we let curb kids
      have our empty pop cans for collection—
karma for the rest of the trip.
Distant mountains stay distant.

(Up the road, don't exit, Phoenix, cartel city)

Instead, turn here for Casa Grande. That's the casino.
It's a walk-rest for seniors, free coffee.
Distant mountains stay distant. Up close, I know
          mountains—that's Camelback.
In a half dream, I want to reach and touch.
The rattlesnake hibernates; we snowbirds migrate.

(This exit, Safeway, Starbucks, organics too.
          Another good pee-stop)

Wal-Mart checkout, a church group with coupons.
Stalled line; we wait. Customer before us
saves pennies, buys processed food, gets diabetes.
Distant mountains stay distant in the front windshield.

(Next exit, Yuma…new territory. I don't know anyone)

My God, they've changed the river's course!
This is a love story about dynamite
          that gave us Imperial Valley
where now a Mexican picker holds
          a globe of lettuce.
Distant mountains stay distant;
          more tall shadows peek beyond them.
The rattlesnake hibernates: we snowbirds migrate.

 Before next exit: Road-block

Our white faces in flashlight,
          waved on.
But the next car, Mexican—
          They live in the skin of the un-chosen.

For them, no exit

The rattlesnake awakens;

we snowbirds migrate.
The distant mountains stay distant
though we push hard to cross the next one.

25. Cinco de Mayo.

Cinco de Mayo Parade

First was the lone Mariachi playing his guitar
and packing pistols.
His belt held, also, his sheath and knife.
He was followed by the brown-robed priests
in back of the mission pick-up, followed too
by the local Catholic group
in its own truck, bannered and proclaiming, *Cristo Rey*.

It was a festive day for the children. The vendors sold
golden horns to play--and drinks of Mexican Orange
made with real sugar, not the American high-fructose stuff.

Best were the 1950s low riders, chopped and channeled,
cars riding formation, some with green, orange, white flags,
and on the hoods, vintage ornaments shining bright.

Followed by a garden of girls in voluptuous dresses
who stepped to the music, their hair shining and adorned
with a profusion of blooms.

This was Cinco de Mayo, Main Street, Arizona,
hot homemade posole, fresh tortillas, fireworks to follow.

∽

All seen longingly
                from the other side
of the Border.

Soldier On

He is a Mexican who was a U.S. soldier
in Iraq, his sad heart a fallen raven,
a tough man around glass dishes.
I made him homemade pizza
with pepperoni, peppers, mushrooms.
He was overjoyed to be welcomed,
to eat warm food at my table.

For him, it was like he was home
with his parents in Mexico, yellow chairs,
dog at his feet, table-talk of laughter.

He said—*I've had enough of guns,*
never again in my lifetime—
Church is a good place for me.

But he is now here in a hard life
of Arizona tricks—roadblocks always
on a highway; harsh flashlight beams
on his Latino face; he passes his license
through the car window.

He is an experienced warrior,
on piece-work wages.

Runners

There they are—at the corner of my eye.
My daughter sees them too
      as we drive across the desert floor.
There, where the mesa shadow marks the rise—
There, three shadow-like spiders against the wall
running in black knit caps, holding black trash bags,
their possessions for the trip. *Runners,* my daughter says.
We wonder, as we near Tucson pushing 80—
if those in the pulse of cars have seen them go
will reach for phones, call border patrol.

Often we see plastic milk jugs at the end of ranch drives
filled with water—or up under bridge concrete, water too,
      plastic measure saving lives
and clothes filled plastic bags, a connection point.
On Sundays, we read the paper. There, always,
a map of Cochise County. Black stars designate
the bodies found—runners not making it, in 110 heat.
Crops won't happen without working hands and feet.

At 5,000 feet, there is a chance. Fifty miles between
the Border and 10 the Interstate. That's three black nights
      not seen in rock peaks
with javelina, big cat, and rattlesnake.
My trailer has an eye-hook to hold the door.
The dogs do their usual yipping under the stars.
Never have we seen a soul. They stay away and run,
knowing we have phones—thinking we have guns.

Sardines

Runners eat sardines.
Sardines and water can get you to Denver.
So I was at the Cheaper Store where
there are the cheapest sardines, not lovely in slim silver lines
when you open the can, but a big, lumpy bargain.

I was one step ahead at the sardine shelf.
There were three, "runners" I guessed,
boots caked, Mexican faces with dark beard, dirt
wrinkled—no English, please.
They gave me a bow, deferred to me, grandmother,
shyly stepped back. And for my part
in exchanged courtesy, I took but two cans of sardines.
Their eyes said, *Yes,* a tremor in their hands,
and they cleaned out the shelf.

You pay cash at the Cheaper Store, and I went first in line.
They nodded as gentlemen do, and then outside,
I hurried to my old VW, beat up, unlocked, ready to ride.
They smiled as they came out, and I smiled too.
I had my fair share. Two cans of sardines would do.

And I remember once in Paris at the Metro,
our crowd pushed back to the wall
away from the platforms—and I smelled sardines.
I looked over my shoulder, and there he was
a man eating sardines with a toothpick from a can.
I knew it!—I cried. *Sardines.* And to my surprise
he answered in English…Wisconsin in France!
And at that moment, I longed for a can of sardines.
So it is now. All of us on the move. I wish all travelers well
for I am in motion too, moving through the present tense
like quicksilver
       across a slanted,
           pull-out, trailer table.
     I have a paper plate, bread, sardines.

26. Gruene, Texas.

Piñata

Texas drought—here for many months.
Wildfires everywhere
burn at the edges of our eyes
beyond the subdivisions.
We pray—the Catholic and the Baptist
       together.

And then, leaving the grocery, we hear
       rumble on the horizon
and see legions
       of advancing clouds—like angels.

Then overhead—Sumo giants;
       elephants filling with water;
       polar bears clinging to dripping ice.
Clouds stream above us, windswept heavy weights
       bellies sagging all day.

At hazy sunset, the first drops come.
Mist from hot pavement surrounds us.
We walk from beneath trees to open lawn,
cool silvered water on our foreheads.

We cup our palms like leaves,
       thirsty,
children beneath a piñata.

Somewhere there will be tornados,
       lightning striking wires,
dogs, cats, and cars awash in rising arroyos.

But here, our necks crane backward.
This is charmed celebration.
We take a long walk about the wet grass,
wave to a compadre—out too—in the falling rain.

Immigration

My Japanese daughter-in-law brought me along
to see the Austin specialist, so I could help her
          understand...
As always, before you see the big doc,
you are in the room with the nursing assistant,
and your history is reviewed.

Our nurse was male, Latino, his hair pulled slick
into a ponytail, more than one tattoo on his dark arm.
He shuffled the paperwork in his hands,
...*Your name is—Benvenuto?...Italian?*
          I nodded.
...*Benvenuto. That means—welcome?*
I nodded again, pleased he caught the meaning.

He gave us a long look weighing
our un-Italian looks, my red, sandy hair,
Junko's almond eyes,
          so I opened the door,
...*I'm Irish, but I married an Italian,*
so my son is Benvenuto, and he has married
Junko, here, and now she is Benvenuto too...

His smiled flashed, wondering at the two of us.
...*Ahh, well, as it should be...*
          Beautiful
And then he said—*They are political borders anyway.*

He added, *My name is Coronado.*
...*Ahh,* I replied—*the famous explorer,*
looking for the city of gold,
and have you found the city of gold?
          We both laughed.

Later, in the car, my daughter-in-law asked,
...*What were you and the man talking about?*

I told her it was our name,
how the two of us, she and I, came to be called
Welcome.

27. Posing in front of LBJ Air Force One.

Even the Fortune Cookies are in Spanish
(at the Border Chinese food stand)

The minute I thought of you
Jimi Hendrix came on Classic Rock
and I remembered—
having to buy him on vinyl
and play him on our record player
(because he was censored then,
too dirty to play national airwaves)
while we made love on the worn
gray pattern couch. It was naptime
for all our kids.

&

Today, I was with our four grandchildren
and the fortune cookie
sent a direct message from you to me
Esta buena mi nana pa mi tata—
My Grandma is good for my Grandpa.
They are a perfect match

Which just goes to show
time and borders mean nothing
when heaven is in charge.
Fortune cookies hone the truth,
make us realize—
There is memory in music.
There is memory on our lips.

Mary, Mary, I Am Waiting for Your Tamales

They are the best Christmas gift, and when I get them
I put them in my freezer, so when Juan arrives,
he will be fooled and think I have made them.
Do not let me down. Remember? I told you he was coming
the day you gave me the merengue lesson.
You showed me those tiny smooth steps and to be fly-quick
hipped,
though it was Advil for days after ...

And then—what to wear? You and I picked
through the racks at the Boutique together.
Your arched brows knew exactly what to choose—
the midi-blouse with the Swiss cheese holes,
to bra or not to bra and get away with it…
And then you snapped out
those polka-dot polyester/cotton pants, drapey,
with the sly string waist
that comes loose with one little pull.

> For Juan
> For his Camaro in my drive
> For the click of his boot on my trailer step
> For his witchcraft voice, soft as Texas toast.

No, don't shake your clucking finger at me now. I will be wise.
I still have your hammered tin-can Virgin Mary nailed to my
wall.
I still have the palm leaf frond that you brought
from your visit to your mother's church.
He will see the flames of all my votive candles, and he will
know
that the merengue is all he may get after the tamales,
and that not all chilies are green.

28. Mariachi.

Ode to Jerry Garcia

Ahh, Jerry, now that you have left me
      I can say,
you were the standard by which we lived our time.
You and I are the same age,
and when I was in tie-dye and bell bottoms,
it was your music on the fire escapes at midnight.

When my hair hung to my waist, and I was barefoot,
      it was your music
from the parking lots at the beach.
You were the music of the psychedelic head shops
in Old Town, Chicago—the year of revolution
when the pigs pushed Dan Rather down
      in the aisles
of the Democratic National Convention.

You were the immense music of the Oregon coast
of Ken Kesey weddings when bride and groom
wore long white prayer gowns and daisy chains.
And wedding gifts were six-legged starfish.

In Viet Nam, you were the home comfort
      night watch music
for my cousin, Mike, sitting in a tree
with a rifle ready across his legs
shooting Charlie to the *Lady in Red*
and listening to the sound of Nam voices.
Yes, you were the music of Sai Gon
and the 24-hr. leave—of neon and cocaine
and the must-be-forgotten jungle.

Forest Gump is fiction in all those famous scenes
and probably a Republican, Jerry Garcia,
but you were the genuine coin
that could be traded anywhere—*Dead* tapes,

vendors, street corners, yes.

With you, I was the first generation on the pill
and how we used that freedom.
        Late into the summer night
we would be out on the campus grass erecting
        utopias.
At dawn, I would sleep in my pedestal bathtub,

my toe tips ruling the faucets,
the lone light bulb above me, the roaches
walking away with the wallpaper,
        and I would sing
to you, Jerry Garcia, about *sugar magnolias*
for *I could bath in a dewdrop too.*
And I knew somewhere else—last night's
"hot-time" should be walking in sunbeams.

And then you moved on like we moved on
only to resurface again for my children,
stoned on Led Z and Ozzie, and Greyhound
road trips across the country to camp anywhere,
any parking lot, to be with you for one more
$20 sheet—shawls of colors, pipes of hashish.

And now my daughter has grown up too.
That means both of us have little dead-head decals
faithfully stuck on our hatchback windows—
such a rare mother/daughter bonding.

At the Dead Shop on Clark St. in Chicago,
the guy behind the counter drinks beer
while he rings our sale. At the Dead Shop in E.L.
the air is sweet, and no one cares.
        Ahh, Jerry Garcia,
what you have done for capitalism in America.
You are a millionaire of ice-cream.
Money falls from your fingertips.

You exact the money/music of sweet illusion.

Well, now you are dead. With you closes
the final door to the sixties. How can I tell
        some 15 yr.-old before me—
that I like glass beaded curtains?
(Do you realize, Jerry Garcia, that you and I learned
to drive a car before there was such a thing
as steering column turning signals?)

A solemn, final moment now for a warm Garcia vision.
Watch for an old VW on the painted California rim.
The driver zigzags, going where he pleases
until he gets to the foot of a rainbow
and drives right up the multicolored arch of highway.
...Ahh, Jerry, it wasn't a very long trip at all.

29. Two guitars on the wall.

Part Four
He is a bright dot

30. Road signs.

Home—the Story Ends

Home can be two double-wides shoved together with a bedroom housing more than one sibling and popcorn for supper. Home is a four-letter word that takes paragraphs of words to describe—the connotations go on and on. The concept "home" crosses languages. Home does not depend on size or money, or religion or food choices. Home is where you can be yourself with no pretenses. Home is where you can fart. If there are other people in your home, they feel comfortable to be with even if they annoy you on occasion. They say expected things well received or not. They don't steal your pillow but they may take the "throw" you use on the couch. Home is where you can go after a really bad day. You can forget about the fact that you stutter, or that your peers made you the butt of a joke, or that you were really angry "out there," but now that you are home you can break into the strawberry Twizzlers and be calm again.

But home is also a point in geography. In my case, it is a dot on the landscape on the outskirts of Safford, Arizona. For the tourist, the landscape here is spectacular. The horizon is a perfect flat line crossing the high mesa. A few ancient blasted volcano cones crop up in the distance. The sharp rise of the mountains from the desert floor sometimes takes your breath away as you drive into town. The sunrises and sunsets reflected on the mountain peaks (sometimes snow covered in colors of pink,) give you the feeling that "all's right with the world."

My special landscape has two significant features. The first are the hot springs coming from the 10,720 ft. mountain next to my home. Some people in the neighborhood have springs coming up right on their property. The springs feed several area ponds. The result is abundant wildlife enjoying several miles of oasis in a desert world.

The second feature is the star-scape. Our mountain, Mt Graham, boasts of three world-class telescopes, and below there is an observatory that welcomes visitors every Saturday night. So not only can one learn the names of the celestial bodies from the astronomers, but one can walk nightly under stars which reach from horizon to horizon and seem brighter than anywhere else.

This is my southwestern home. Add to this my daughter and her family, her dogs and cats, her friends—and my friends. My grandson's name is Duncan. This is his father's middle name. The town directly east is Duncan. Everyone I talk to has a story about the town of Duncan. Plus, the mountain next to us was named after a prominent soldier, Lt. Colonel James Duncan Graham in 1846. He was an officer in the Army Corps of Topographical Engineers.

Forty miles south is the railroad. We are caught sometimes by the train at the crossing and have to wait. We watch the rolling of the boxcars as they clack on through. I look for a hobo, but nowadays there are none. Yet somehow the face that would be on the train is now my grandson's face. You can see it in the jaw, the blue of the eyes—but most of all, it's the kid who will take a dare, unafraid; he's skinny but strong. I watch him on his roller blades. He is a bright dot, arms swinging, moving below a tall vast mountain. He is perfectly at home.

31. Boy before mountains.

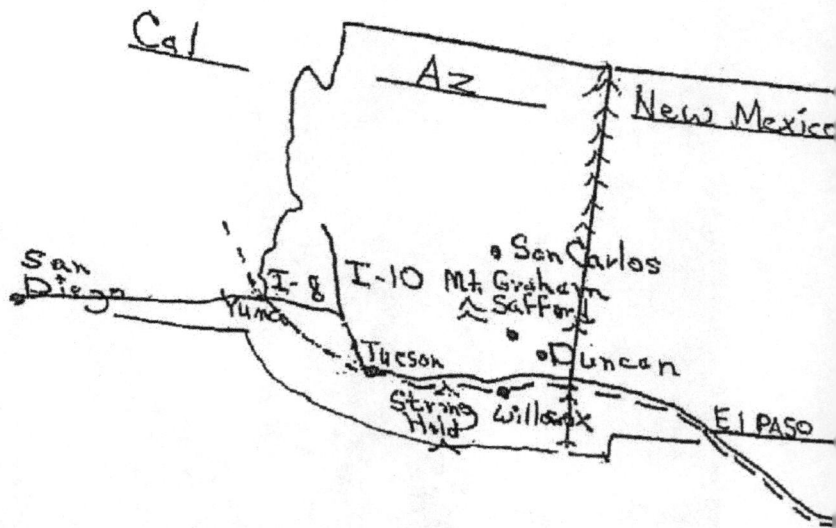

32. Map D: I-10 and the Union Pacific Railroad.

Road

S

AUSTIN   DALLAS

Gruene

San Antone

Fleetwood Trailer

My 37ft Pace Arrow,
      my pod in the desert night.

Above is my galaxy—
      sparks at my fingertips.

33. Fleetwood and white dog.

Arizona Open Road
(Walt Whitman)

The road is open, Cochise Stronghold far ahead.
The car bumps over humps, and we unsettle.
Our hats jog, our sunglasses skew.
      Don't open the windows.
      Air on. Water jug on the floor.

We'll get there, past the Indian outpost and the last post office.
Out to where the bones blow in the wind on fence lines...
      cattle skulls.

We go because it's home out there, a trailer on a dirt track;
a bird feeder calls from a near tree,
      water from a deep well.

At evening, we sit and watch red rock.
Painted clouds streak toward the evening star.
In the night, coyotes quarrel, snarl and snap, howl
      over road-kill in the cooling dust.
Orion gives us time overhead, quietly paces the sky.

First light, jagged purple Chiricahua peaks fill the horizon.
Stars wink and go, and I fill my cup.
      Start the microwave.
Where will we go today? Up, upon the cliffs?
Like lizards up-siding boulders?

Or maybe park our chairs in the gravel driveway,
open our books on glyphs and graphs. Look up occasionally.
In the small speck distance, puff of dust—purr of wheels.
      Someone else on the open road.

Arizona Girls

So I am independent.
That is why I was in a parking lot
taking photos of the distant mountain range
way the hell out in nowhere. My car and me.
…but suddenly, another car, a jeep with a German Shepard
       panting out a back window
and then a woman driver stepped out in jeans,
boots, a leather vest. She gave a nod but then moved
to check her car: opening the hood, raising it with a rag,
twisting this and that. From the back, she brought a jug
       of blue fluid, began to pour.

Watching her work, I started the simple conversation,
Like what are you doing, way out here?

…so she said she was a tracker by trade;
looked for lost folks in the mountains,
sometimes New Mexico, sometimes here,
and the lost are usually found, thanks to the dogs.
       Lost only three people since she began.

Her car check over, she swallowed water, some
for her dog. I watched as off she careened
into the mountain distance. Wondering…
       why'd she pull in next to my car…?
       Was she worried about me?
Or maybe—she was alone on the road,
and seeing another car, another woman—our sisterhood,
       safety.

Birth of a Grandson

You come in a summer drought
      but feed the spring.
In you is generation, and the old among us rejoice.
We dance around waving our gin and tonics.
We wax long on old stories
We spend money on a lot of food.

For in you—is celebration;
like Buddha, you are a mystery.
Where do you come from?
…in your infinite ways—
      you know.
Without knowing, you know…
how to lift your arm and reach
      and touch my wondering lips.
Where do you come from?

And since, we, in our long lives
cannot answer that question, we sleep well,
knowing great mysteries remain.

Belonging to Constellations
(after Walt Whitman)

I don't mind walking beneath the stars,
      the vault of night.
My feet crunch the gravel drive
but my eyes look upward naming stars
that move with pendulum grace from east to west
as reoccurring as tomorrow's news.

Aren't you afraid? Others have said,
to walk about in the desert night?
Afraid of what? I've thought...
      Coyotes howl;
a star shoots across the sky,
the first bird still hours away
--snakes—safely sleep in the frosty cold.

The walk makes me feel I am in a constellation
      of my own—
the big house holding those I love,
my trailer orbiting like a happy moon,
cars in the drive,
dogs asleep in the oleander bush,
quail tucked like Seven Sisters inside a tree.

Our pattern hums beneath the patterns in the sky
and each night, I join the eternal watchman.
        I walk and remark
        this night in time.

Starry Night

Arizona stars pour
from your fingertips
—like your breath pouring
from your mouth, pouring stars.
Your mouth, your breasts
are filled with stars too.

No need to be on a mountaintop.
You can be at your doorstep,
your key still in the turning lock,
and you find
stars on your right shoulder
filling your purse.

How can you go inside
when the night is more glorious
than sun-lizard days—
or your beckoning room
in lamplight.

One minute more…
Walk along the rock path
beaming upward…

where stars pour
from your fingertips.
Give them a name…*Serenity*
or maybe *Beatitude*
or just *Squashblossom.*
Shape them
into your own constellation.
Mark them

for your grandchildren.

Mountain Time

An ordinary kitchen, an ordinary life—quite so.
Beyond the window, the mountains are 8,000 ft
--and between the two,
on the high mesa, pottery shards
        of ancient tribes.

The mountains keep their own time, free of plans,
        maps, calculations.
They have seen generations of mountain cats,
        and iridescent flies.

These mountains will have seen more when
this once modern kitchen is old,
when the children of these who will become ancestors
themselves ask—
        What to do
what to do—with this old adobe, sun
                        and wind-scraped, home?

Improving on Walt Whitman

When I heard the learn'd astronomer tell us about Orion,
and the new stars being born
in the nebula below his three star belt,
and when I looked through the bathtub size telescope
      to see the four milky stars,
I was delighted to be in this place on this night.

We were in the outdoor amphitheater
at Mt Graham—an observatory
below a sweep of desert sky.
There the gentle youthful astronomer pointed
to various brilliant spots with his lazar star pointer.
Ah, it was splendid to be here. I could not walk away.

That there are young men still, so scholarly, they quietly spend
their nights amongst the officiating stars;
that there are still places so unmindful of wired illumination
that the noble skies are in full command,
      and we are the sole few watchers.

Javalina
(wild desert pigs)

Birds in a tree singing, *seed, feed,*
busy Epiphany sunset welcoming
in the new year.
In the night, squeals in the landscape,
javalina are waiting in the wash.
They too want to eat the seed block.

But this time, we've got 'em.
We've tucked it up in the fork
of desert oak branches for our birds,
and now the flock of quail is happy:
the cardinal too,
the Gila woodpecker.
They sing all evening long
while we sit on porch chairs, drink lemonade.

At ground level, the roadrunner scurries.
The dogs sleep curled, no pigs to chase now.
Meanwhile, back in the ravine—
the javalina reconvene.
They will get the seed block.
Their smiles belie the contest
            between.

Ida's Room

The pond fed by the mountain
has warm spring water,
warm in the cool Arizona morn.
      Mallards abound…
and black coots with white beaks.
Ducks—their red feet caught
in sunshine—fly above the pond.

Trees grow tall: the emperor palms,
      the date palm, the cedars,
their roots set in ample water dreams.

This is Ida's room
a grand lady for 97 years,
and I am in it now for sleeping easy.
What a friend—lady of the mountain.
She dug the pond; she planted the trees;
she shared with us
      abundant warm water,
      her life pleasant, and long.

Indoors and outdoors,
      it's…
            Ida's room.

It Feels Good to Lie Down in My Bones

The desert heat melts my marrow.
I am a dry something or other
hanging from bones.

My bones look back at me
from a shelf on my wall.
They tell me—no more need
for dental implants.
That's past tense now.
No need for sealing windows
from dust storms.
Dust is calling the meeting to order.
No need for alarm clocks.
Alarm left months ago,
right after Destiny, duo in the pale sunset.

It's me only
sitting on hipbones,
turning on neck bones,
writing with bent knuckles.

At the End of Time

At the end, will they still be playing Classic Rock?
Will paper plates still have holiday theme decorations?
Will Dr. Scholl's foot reverie
                        still be a pharmacy mainstay?

At the end of time, will our rivers run uphill?
Will sheep turn on the wolf
                        and eat him for breakfast?
Will the root that we brew into tea
            send signal dreams to our fingertips?

How soon is the end of time?

If I stand in the shadow of the rock
                        on the mountaintop,
        Will I find it?
Or will I hear only Classic Rock
                        played on a car radio
in a campground down below...
two lovers turning the wheel slightly
                        with the nudge of their heat...
the soles of their feet
            for the moment, gone from the earth.

The Road to Duncan

I can see it from the drive, the break in the mountain ridge,
the marker rock edifice says: the road east is here,
the slow rise of red wash land to New Mexico
        and the Continental Divide.

I have been to Duncan, a geographical dot on high desert,
a welcome green road along the Gila River, cottonwoods.
Where nowadays a board store—sells wellness crystals
along with fuel pumps from past times that advertise lead gas.
The long flatbed trucks take turns slowly in this old west town.
They hold bright sheets of copper coming down from the mine.

            ∾

My grandson's name is Duncan, youngest male
in the continuing line. He and his dad try Gila
canyon adventures; following stream to rock pool
where they strip and swim; talk caution to each other
about rattlesnakes or big cat...
Here, Duncan learns new trails in wilderness.

They are hungry now
        and stop for food in Duncan...
burgers and fries before the way home.

            ∾

Unlike Duncan's great-grand father, the railroad bum,
hungry for days, though forever traveling west from Texas,
through New Mexico, riding train cars,
his eye on these same mountains
looking for those marker rocks, the "v" in the rim
that tell him legendary tales of hidden Apache
        behind towering boulders
in wait for the stage—the drivers, the shotguns,
        the passengers—in flight for their lives.

Some will find it ... the way through.

34. Poet with grandson Duncan, about 7,000 ft on
Mount Graham.

35. Egret.

End Notes

10-The Interstate: Poetic License—Neither Hatch, N.M. nor Yuma, Az are on Interstate-10.

"And many have entertained Angels, unaware," is a quote from Hebrews 13:2.

Chiricahua Mountains National Park, Az: This is the historic home of the Chiricahua Apache. The road over the mountains takes you from the New Mexico border to the mountain peak known as Dos Cabezas. The Apache were moved by the U.S. government 50 miles north to the San Carlos Rez.

Cochise. This poem is in the form of Native American storytelling.

Cochise Stronghold, Az is a box canyon. Cochise put his men up on the rocks at the entrance to guard, so the canyon was a safe place for families. The Apache return here each year to celebrate their renowned ancestor.

Duncan, Az is a lonely spot on the high desert. It is halfway between Safford and Interstate 10. It is on the banks of the Gila River. The railroad runs along the road. This is where a second road drops down from the copper mines. So if you need food or gas, you are safe if you can get to Duncan.

Dragoon, Az: Of note are the ruins of the stagecoach station up in the hills. The graves of the soldiers who defended the station against the Apache are still there.

Fort Bowie, Az: It was built to hold back the Apache. You can visit the historic site. On the trail to the fort is Apache Spring. Also on the way is the site where Cochise cut his way out of the tent. This is close to the site of the pony express.

Gandy Dancer: According to my dictionary, a gandy dancer is a laborer in a railroad section gang.

Gruene, Tx: They have not torn down the dance hall. Musicians still play there. Stevie Ray Vaughn has played there. The dancing goes on today.

History: The steering-column turning signal began in the 1950s. Before that, the driver's window was rolled down and the arm extended. Extending the arm straight out indicated a left-turn. Holding the arm and hand upright meant the driver was turning right.

Rattlesnake Crafts Az: Allow here for poetic imagination. Rattlesnake Crafts did not exist in the 1920s, nor is it located next to the siding in Willcox. This is where a poet finds an incredible image and has to fit it into a poem somewhere even if she moves it 50 miles away and changes the decade. The real Rattlesnake Crafts was along the Old Ghost Town Road along the Border.

The Three Sisters, Az: The three mountain peaks are a symbol of the San Carlos Rez. You know you are coming into San Carlos when you see the peaks.

The Triangle-T property in Az has been owned since the 1920s, so my dad may have been camping on someone's land. Nevertheless, the rocks known as Texas Canyon have been there for eons, so my dad may have been beside any formidable rock. The area can be walked now. Historically, the property has been used for movie sets.

A Photo Story of the *Road to Duncan*

All photographs were taken by the poet. Interior photos have been remastered and rendered in black and white.

Cover: Train over desert along I-10.

Southwest Intro photos: Poet's mom and dad taken Sept. 13, 1931, married 1 year and 2 months. Buck was in his swimming outfit. It was improper for a man to expose his bare chest in those days.

San Xavier Mission, south of Tucson and south of I-10

Lizard photographed at the Desert Museum, Tucson

36. Pass to Duncan.

First Section—Riding the Rails

Buck retired around age 65.
A boxcar at the Austin Steam Train tracks, Cedar Park, TX
Cowboys at the Triangle-T, Dragoon, AZ.
Longhorn bronze, Dallas, TX.
Railroad Crossing at the Coronado Vineyards, AZ.
Hobo art peach pit carved by Lee shown here on an Apache medicine purse.

37. Mountain lion.

Second Section—The Apache Story

Rock pillar formation in Chiricahua Mountains National Park.
Gaan dancer doing the dance of the Mountain Spirits beneath Three Sisters Mountain.
Woman of Eleven Horses.
Fancy dancers at a Pow-Wow, San Carlos Casino Resort.
Traveling into the San Carlos Rez on Rt. 90.

Third Section—Travelers, the Border Story

Inn at Castle Rock, Bisbee, AZ
Offerings at San Xavier Mission, Tucson, AZ.
Truck along the Old West Highway going to Duncan.
Cinco de Mayo Parade, Safford, AZ.
Gruene Dance Hall, oldest dancehall in Texas.
Daughter-in-law in front of Lyndon Johnson's Air Force One on display at his ranch.
Mariachi with pistol and guitar—Safford Cinco de Mayo parade
Display found along back porch wall, Safford, AZ.

Fourth Section—Home, the Story Ends

Road signs in Duncan, AZ.
Boy skateboarding at fairgrounds, Gila Mountains, Safford, AZ.
Poet's trailer, a Fleetwood, 37ft Pace Arrow, below Cochise Stronghold, AZ.
Poet with grandson Duncan, about 7,000 ft on Mt Graham.

Closing Notes

Egret at Ida's pond, Graham Apartments, Safford, AZ.

Photo Story

Pass to Duncan rock formation as seen from Roper Lake State Park, Az.
Mountain lion taken at the Desert Museum, Tucson, AZ.
Hilda's Restaurant in Duncan, AZ.

38. Hilda Restaurant, Duncan, AZ.

Photo Index

Acknowledgements

First of all I would like to thank my two readers, Jim Eriksen and Kathy Fedewa. They were kind enough to read all my words and to give me new insight into my own work. This book is better because they read it first.

Secondly, I have had the privilege of working with other poets— Anne McCabe, Ruelaine Stokes, and Brandon Knight to name three. Again, my work is better because of their response. And, like other poets, I live in writing groups. From each, I glean a little more self-awareness of my own work. The first are the women of Michigan State University's Writing Group. Some of them have followed me for thirty years. The second is a little group that meets in Williamston's Tavern 109. They too have been a great audience. Poet, Mary Anna Kruch leads this group. The beer on tap is good too.

But more so, I have been delighted to find a Western audience for my work—my audience at Mt. Graham Apartments; the Hargis family; the Walker family; and the Apache themselves. Every time I have a conversation, I've learned a little more about my own poetry and how it finds a place in the hearts of others.

❧

But there are others who helped me tell my tales. I have put them in alphabetical order, so they can find their names quickly—

Cristi, my patient, personal computer guru. She made this all happen.

Doug McCausland. Doug and I worked together to put *Hop a Train* to musical composition.
It can be heard at www.soundcloud.com/doug-mccausland-1. Since it was done two years ago, you will have to scroll down Doug's file to find it.

Ethlene Philips, the best Apache cook ever. We began with recipes. That started the conversation. Ethlene makes acorn soup and sets the standard for fry bread.

Gary Kelly, my brother and son of Buck. Gary and I have traded our stories back and forth for years. He knew that Buck was sentenced to 30 days in the El Paso Jail.

Grateful Dead allusions: *Lady in Red, Sugar Magnolias, Bathing in Dewdrops, Long Trip After All.*

Ida Lukats: After Ida died at 97, I was allowed to stay in her room which I did for more than one visit. Some of the poems in this book were written in Ida's room. There is a pond outside her window where many birds can be observed. When sitting outside near the water, the mountains rise up in close view.

John (old John) McLean. I did not know it as I sat and talked with him that this was the last year of his life. I took notes, but now I so wish I could have asked him even more about the railroad.

Juliet Walker, my daughter: She introduced me to the West. I live in the West because she lives in the West. As we drive, we talk endlessly. She was with me as I traveled to various places.

Junko Benvenuto, my daughter-in-law, has generously allowed herself to be the subject of a poem. She and my son live in Austin, Texas, so each year, I am in Texas too.

Nancy Stowe, daughter of Ida: She doesn't know it, but she is running a writer's retreat.

Phyllis Webster, the woman of eleven horses: She has shared her stories with me.

Valerie Kelly. She too has put Buck's tales into poetry. As a high school student she would sit at Buck's feet and ask him to tell her stories. She wrote them down.

Walt Whitman. *Song of the Open Road, When I Heard the Learn'd Astronomer, Song of Myself.* Heritage Press. New York.

Wes Hargis. Wes has put two of my poems into wonderful color prints—*Belonging to Constellations* and *Hop a Train.*

Prior Publication

"Blue Denim," and "Friends with Bones." *Creosote*. Eastern Arizona College. Thatcher, Arizona. June 2018.

"Detroit—1952," was originally published as "Train Tracks" in *A Grand River*, Thunder Bay Press, Holt, MI, 2013.

Hobo poems were first read at the Southwest Cowboy Poetry Festival in Sierra Vista, Arizona, 2007.

"Hop a Train." The poet and Doug McCausland. www.soundcloud.com/doug-mcclausland-1. March 2016.

"Hop a Train" and "Belonging to Constellations" were put into art prints. Wes Hargis, artist. February 2019.

"I Found a Woman," and "Soldier On." *English Language Journal of Michigan*.
Michigan. June 2018.

Sources

In Arizona, I have lived in three areas in the past 20 years. The first is on San Carlos Lake on the San Carlos Rez. The second is at the foot of Cochise Stronghold. The nearby community is called Sunsites. The third is the Safford area itself.

Thus, southeastern Arizona is the setting for most of my poems. Therefore, most of my information comes from me being on site and talking to others who live there.

However, to confirm some of the things I thought I knew, I have read the following sources.

Aleshire, Peter. *Cochise: The Life and Times of the Great Apache Chief.* Wiley. Cabin Fever Books: 2001.

Haley, James L. *The Kings of San Carlos.* Doubleday. New York: 1987. This is the story of the Apache Indians and the Indian agent, John Clum. Its genre is a Double D Western.

Ratje, John. History of Mount Graham. http://mgio.arizona.edu/history—mount-graham. April 17, 2017.

www.ingramcontent.com/pod-product-compliance
Lightning Source LLC
Chambersburg PA
CBHW022027090426
42739CB00006BA/324